013

MATT
FOR DADS

MATTHEW PRITCHETT

studied at St Martin's School of Art in London and first saw himself published in the *New Statesman* during one of its rare lapses from high seriousness. He has been the *Daily Telegraph*'s front-page pocket cartoonist since 1988. In 1995, 1996, 1999, 2005 and 2009 he was the winner of the Cartoon Arts Trust Award and in 1991, 2004 and 2006 he was 'What the Papers Say' Cartoonist of the Year. In 1996, 1998, 2000, 2008 and 2009 he was the *UK Press Gazette* Cartoonist of the Year. Matt recently won the Political Humour/Satire category for *The Best of Matt 2012* at the Political Book Awards. In 2002 he received an MBE.

Own your favourite Matt cartoons. Browse the full range of Matt cartoons and buy online at www.telegraph.co.uk/photographs or call 020 7931 2076.

The Daily Telegraph

MATT
FOR DADS

'It's paternity leave, stop calling it house arrest'

First published in Great Britain in 2013 by Orion Books
A division of the Orion Publishing Group Ltd
Orion House
5 Upper Saint Martin's Lane
London, WC2H 9EA

A Hachette UK Company

10 9 8 7 6 5 4 3 2 1

A CIP catalogue record for this book is available
from the British Library.

ISBN: 978 1 4091 2955 4

Printed in the UK by Cayfosa

The Orion Publishing Group's policy is to use papers that are natural,
renewable and recyclable products and made from wood grown in
sustainable forests. The logging and manufacturing processes are
expected to conform to the environmental regulations of the country
of origin.

www.orionbooks.co.uk

FOR MY FATHER

'At some time in the
next few weeks you're going
to see Daddy cry ...'

'We couldn't afford to
keep the family car'

'Don't kiss it better. I want
you to refer me to a
personal injury lawyer'

'The politicians promised
us that only our children
would suffer'

'We're worried about your
finances and we'd like to
withdraw our pocket money'

'It looked like Santa's grotto –
how was I meant to know it
was a gay wedding?'

'I shall now attempt
to fail a GCSE'

'We know you're upset, Dad,
but please, please, please
don't start dancing'

'Your pocket money is for
sweets – you weren't
meant to buy a house'

'Hello, little baby, you're
billions of pounds in debt'

'Congratulations, son, you've turned from a boy into a suspected paedophile'

'Strikes have closed schools, forcing many parents to take their children to work'

'Half of you got the homework right, half didn't do it and the other half got it wrong'

Parenting

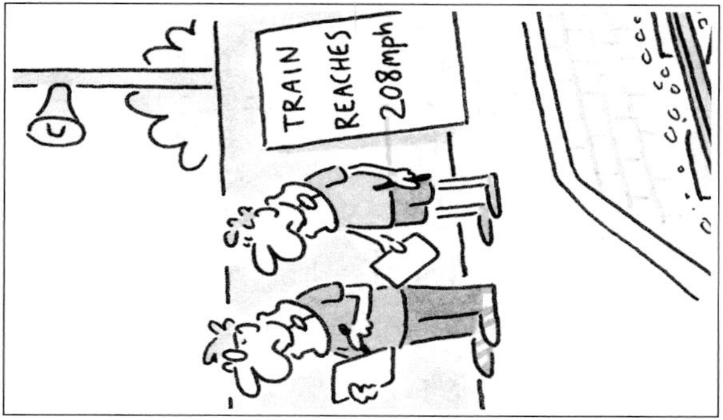
TRAIN
REACHES
208mph

'I said I'm scared!
I don't want a teddy,
I want a loaded gun'

Parenting

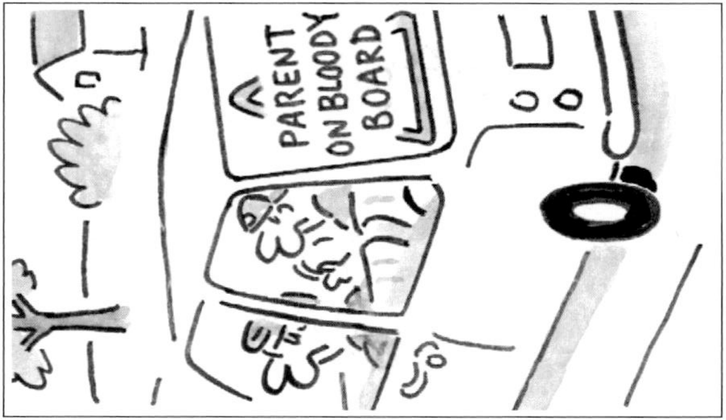
PARENT
ON BLOODY
BOARD

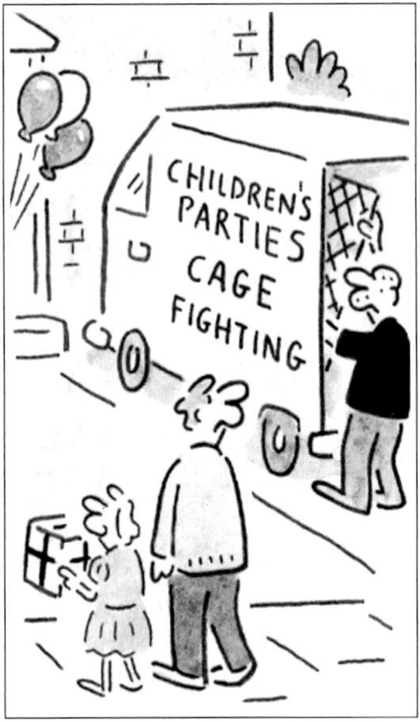
CHILDREN'S
PARTIES
CAGE
FIGHTING

'It's no good, I can't stop
thinking about
Jonny Wilkinson'

Sport

'We beat the West Indies in
1969 and AGAIN this year
it's getting to be monotonous'

'I'm afraid he's in
a meeting'

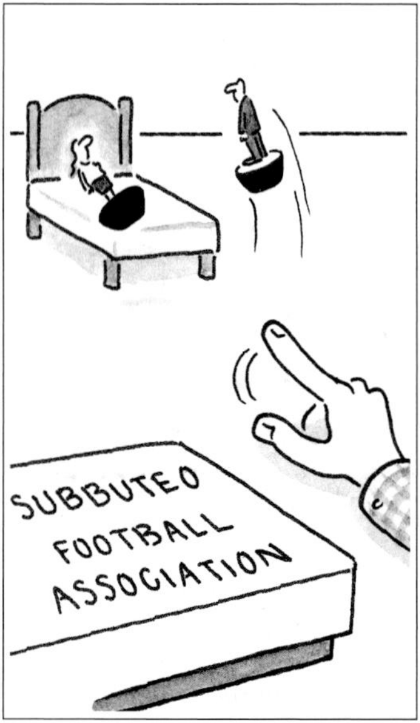
SUBBUTEO
FOOTBALL
ASSOCIATION

'If anyone here present
knows of the score in the
England-Portugal match,
let him speak now...'

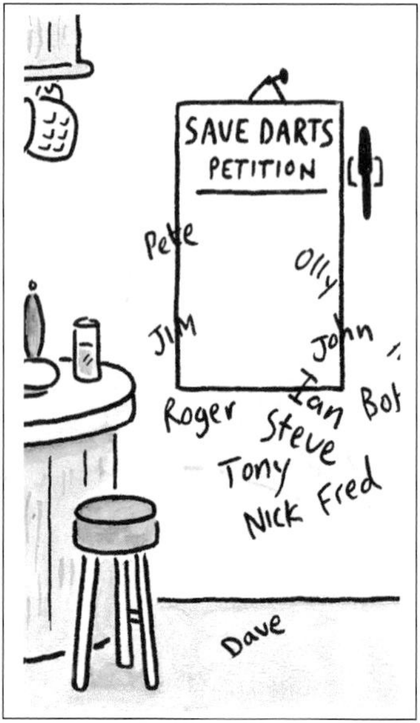
SAVE DARTS
PETITION
Pete
Olly
JIM
John
Roger
Ian
Steve
Tony
Nick
Fred
Dave

'It can't be wrong, it's
guided by satellites'

'Hello, I recently insured
my dog with you...'

'I'm just ringing to say my test is going brilliantly'

'I'm arresting you for
conspiracy to exceed
the speed limit'

Motoring

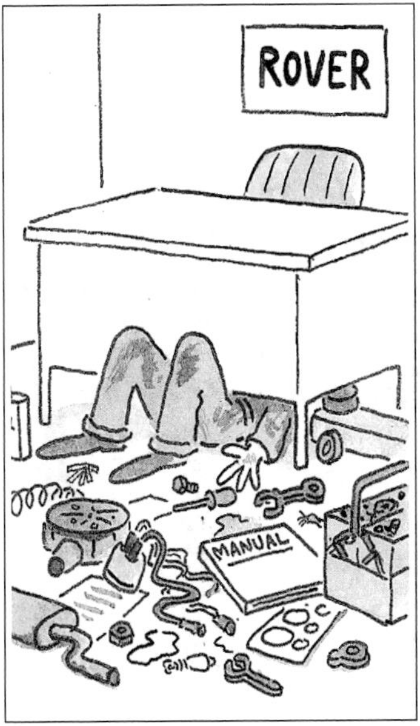
ROVER
MANUAL

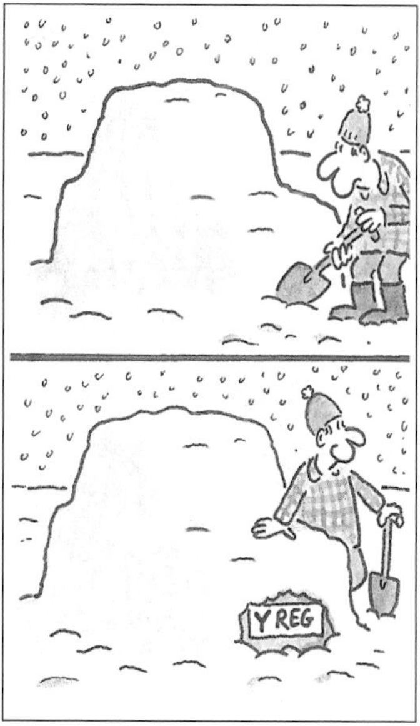
Y REG

'Cheer up, mate, there are plenty more fish in the ... well, cheer up anyway'

'Are there any more like
you at home'

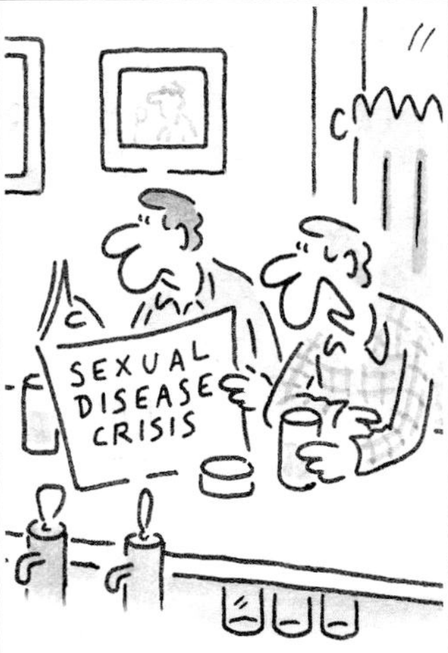
SEXUAL
DISEASE
CRISIS

'I'm trying to look worried, but who am I kidding?'

'You can always tell the
females – they have the
smaller salaries'

'When you said my husband
would be a guinea pig . . .'

'Do we have to pay extra?
My husband has a lot of
emotional baggage'

'Let's invite your
family for Christmas'

'Ladies and gentlemen,
we're very close to creating
the ideal human being'

'My alcohol intake? Well, it's a bit early for me, but I'll have a gin and tonic'

'I can never remember –
does one reduce it by a
third or a half on the form?'

'A liquid bomb – and make
it a double'

'I never have more
than one glass'

'Have you finished
with the Government's
wellbeing survey'

'That's the most impressive
case of bird flu I've ever seen'

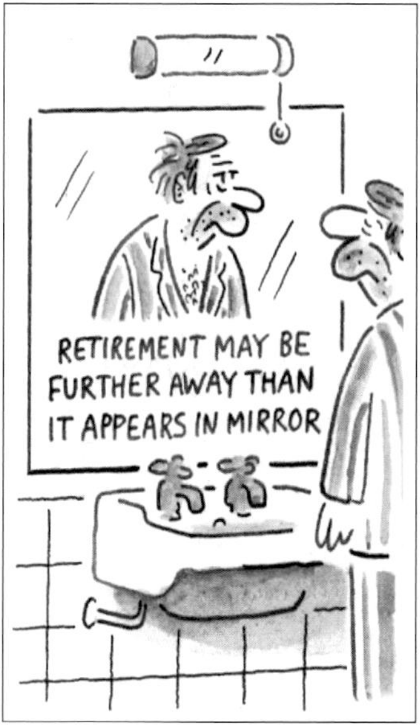
RETIREMENT MAY BE
FURTHER AWAY THAN
IT APPEARS IN MIRROR

'What do we want?
Why did we come here?
What were we saying?'

'Gentlemen, the company
has undergone some changes
since our last board meeting'

'To be honest I just follow
the rest of the market'

'They didn't have any money'

'How much is this house?
.........And how much is
it now?'

Property

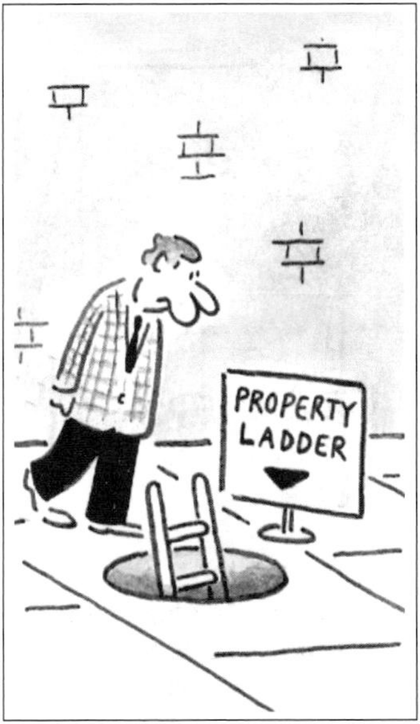
PROPERTY
LADDER

'GAY? I suppose that
means I'll have to pay
for your wedding!'

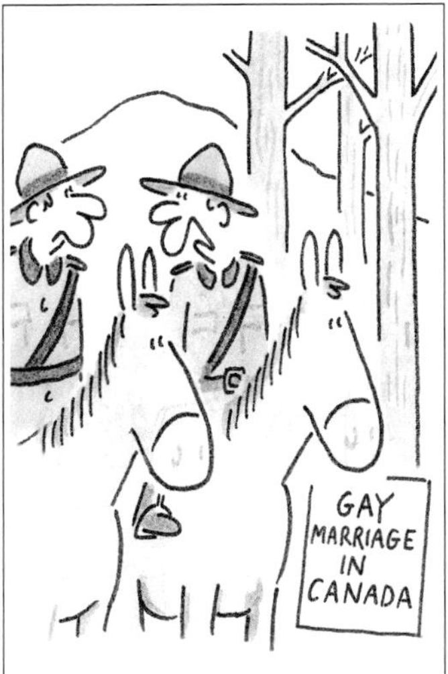
GAY
MARRIAGE
IN
CANADA

'We always get our man'

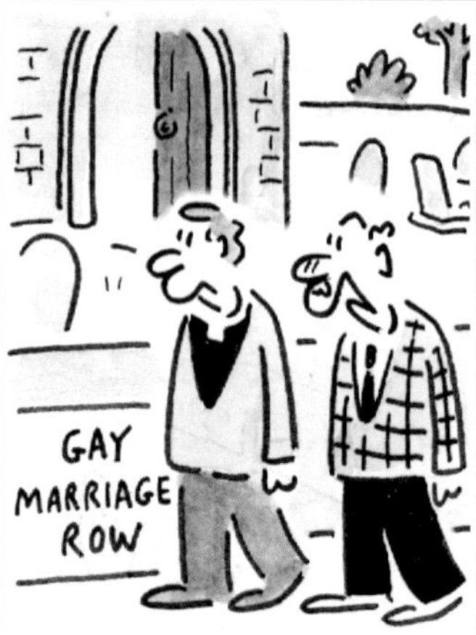
GAY
MARRIAGE
ROW

'I'm a traditionalist. I still believe one of the people getting married should be pregnant'

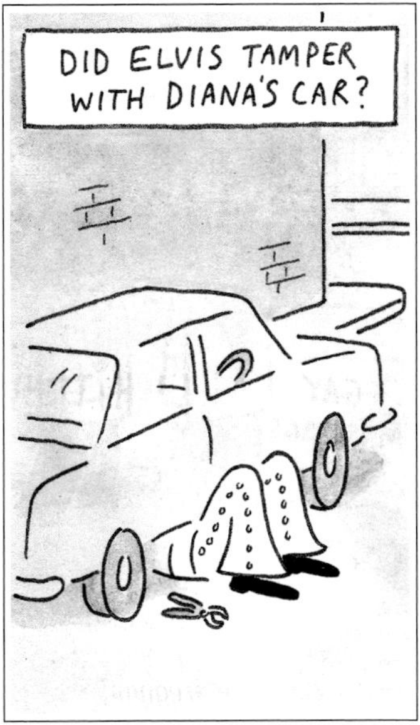
DID ELVIS TAMPER WITH DIANA'S CAR?

'We were hoping you
were going to sing'

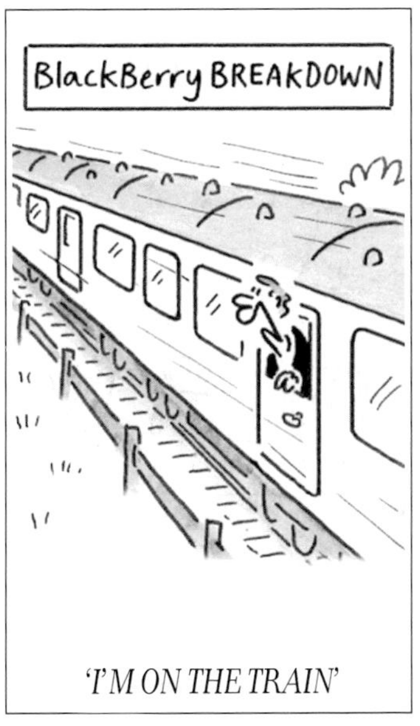
BlackBerry BREAKDOWN

'I'M ON THE TRAIN'

'Hello, love, I'll be late home,
I've caught the train'

'It's much cheaper if you travel at a different time – the 1950s for example'

'Day return?
Feeling lucky, sir?'